W9-DET-069

NATIONAL LEAGUE CENTRAL

By John Silbaugh

THE CHICAGO CUBS, THE CINCINNATI REDS, THE HOUSTON ASTROS, THE MILWAUKEE BREWERS, THE PITTSBURGH PIRATES, AND THE ST. LOUIS CARDINALS

Published in the United States of America by
The Child's World®
PO Box 326 • Chanhassen, MN 55317-0326
800-599-READ • www.childsworld.com

PHOTO CREDITS
Cover: Getty Images
Interior: AP/Wide World: 5, 10, 18, 19, 39, 40; Corbis: 7, 9, 15, 20, 30, 34, 36; Getty Images: 2, 6, 12, 13, 16, 23, 24, 25, 27, 28, 32, 35, 41

ACKNOWLEDGMENTS
The Child's World®: Mary Berendes, Publishing Director

Manuscript and photo research by the Shoreline Publishing Group, LLC

The Design Lab: Kathleen Petelinsek, Design and Page Production

LIBRARY OF CONGRESS CATALOGING-IN-PUBLICATION DATA
Silbaugh, John.
National League Central / by John Silbaugh.
p. cm. — (Behind the plate)
Includes bibliographical references and index.
ISBN-13: 978-1-59296-840-4 (library bound: alk. paper)
ISBN-10: 1-59296-840-6 (library bound: alk. paper)
1. National League of Professional Baseball Clubs—History—Juvenile literature. 2. Baseball teams—United States—Juvenile literature. I. Title.
GV875.A3S55 2007
796.357'640973—dc22 2006029257

The St. Louis Cardinals won the the World Series in 2006, continuing their role as the most successful team in the division.

Contents

INTRODUCTION

The National League (NL) Central Division is very young, having been around only since 1994. But that doesn't mean that the six teams that compose the division are lacking in tradition—far from it. In fact, you'd be hard-pressed to find as many colorful story lines anywhere in baseball as you'll find among the teams in the NL Central.

There's the Chicago curse that often is blamed for keeping the Cubs out of the World Series for more than half a century . . . The "Big Red Machine" that rolled over opponents of the Cincinnati Reds in the 1970s . . . The "Gashouse Gang" that helped the St. Louis Cardinals to the top of the baseball world in the 1940s . . . And lots more.

Indeed, teams such as the NL Central's Chicago Cubs, Cincinnati Reds, Pittsburgh Pirates, and St. Louis Cardinals are among the oldest and most storied franchises in the majors. Along with the Houston Astros and the Milwaukee Brewers, these six clubs have produced some of baseball's greatest teams and greatest individuals.

First, a quick primer on how the NL Central

NATIONAL LEAGUE CENTRAL TEAMS:

Chicago Cubs
Founded: 1874
Park: Wrigley Field
Park Opened: 1914
Colors: Blue and red

Cincinnati Reds
Founded: 1869
Park: Great American Ballpark
Park Opened: 2003
Colors: Red and black

Houston Astros
Founded: 1962
Park: Minute Maid Park
Park Opened: 2000
Colors: Navy blue, burnt orange, and pale yellow

Milwaukee Brewers
Founded: 1969
Park: Miller Park
Park Opened: 2001
Colors: Midnight blue and gold

Pittsburgh Pirates
Founded: 1882
Park: PNC Park
Park Opened: 2001
Colors: Black and gold

St. Louis Cardinals
Founded: 1876
Park: Busch Stadium
Park Opened: 2006
Colors: Cardinal red and navy blue

The Cincinnati Reds back-to-back World Series championship teams of 1975-76 were known as the "Big Red Machine."

8

came to be. In the early 1990s, the league's 14 teams were divided into two divisions, with seven teams in the East and seven teams in the West. When the NL realigned into three divisions in 1994, the Cubs, Pirates, and Cardinals came over from the NL East and the Reds and Astros moved from the NL West to form the new five-team NL Central. At the time, the Brewers played in the American League (AL).

In 1998, baseball expanded with the addition of the AL's Tampa Bay Devil Rays and the NL's Arizona Diamondbacks. But that meant there were 15 teams in each league. An odd number wouldn't work, or else every day there would be one team that couldn't play. To get each league to an even number, the AL's Milwaukee Brewers shifted to the NL Central. Since then, the division has remained the same.

Now, read on about the individual franchises in one of the most exciting divisions in baseball.

Jeff Cirillo was a key hitter for the 1998 Milwaukee Brewers when that team joined the NL Central for the first time.

CHAPTER ONE

THE CHICAGO CUBS

If ever a team was due for a championship, it's Chicago. The Cubs have not won a World Series title since 1908—almost 100 years! They have a rich and colorful history, and they play in one of the most beautiful ballparks in the country, but a string of heartbreaks has kept them from the top.

The most recent example of that came in 2003, when the Cubs won a thrilling NL Central chase before beating the Atlanta Braves in the Division Series for their first postseason win in 58 years. Then, after building a three-games-to-one lead against Florida in the NL Championship

The "friendly confines" of Wrigley Field in Chicago have been the home of the Chicago Cubs and their legions of loyal fans since 1916.

Series (NLCS), they took a 3–0 lead into the eighth inning of Game 6 at home. But they let the game and, eventually, the NL **pennant**, slip away.

Maybe it all has to do with "The Curse." Here's how the story goes: The Cubs were in the World Series in 1945. As a publicity stunt, a local business owner tried to bring a goat into Wrigley Field for one of the games against the Detroit Tigers. The ticket takers, of course, would not allow it. So the man put a curse on the Cubs, vowing they would never again win the World Series. And you know what? They haven't. Cubs fans may or may not believe in the curse, but it sure does represent a change in fortunes from when the club was a powerhouse in the early years of the 20th century. Chicago first began playing in the National Association in 1874 and 1875 as the Chicago White Stockings. After becoming a **charter member** of the NL in 1876, they had at least 16 different nicknames, including the Orphans, the Colts, and the Remnants. In 1902, the club underwent a major rebuilding: As many as 20 rookies were on the roster. A local sportswriter dubbed the young squad "the Cubs." The name stuck and was officially adopted five years later.

Cubs teams of the early 1900s featured a famous double-play combination. The trio of shortstop Joe Tinker, Johnny Evers, and Frank Chance was immortalized in a famous poem:

These are the saddest
of possible words,
Tinker to Evers to Chance. . .
Making a Giant hit into a
double,
Words that are heavy with
nothing but trouble,
Tinker to Evers to Chance.

The Cubs scored a run here during Game 6 of the 1945 World Series, but like every other chance they had from 1908 through 2006, they came up short and didn't earn a title.

11
CUBS

In 1906, the Cubs won a major-league record 116 games before losing to the crosstown White Sox in the World Series. That was just a temporary setback, however, because the Cubs returned to beat the Detroit Tigers for the crown in 1907 and 1908. They were the first back-to-back World Series champions in baseball history. Those championship teams featured one of the best pitchers of the era in Mordecai "Three Finger" Brown. He won 20 games or more in six straight seasons and added four World Series wins from 1906 to 1908.

Moredecai "Three-Finger" Brown lost parts of two fingers in a farming accident, but the accident turned him into a Hall of Fame pitcher.

Wrigley Field did not have lights until 1998. Though night baseball was introduced to the majors in the 1930s, Cubs fans saw all their games in the daylight for 72 years. On August 8, 1988, the lights finally came on at Wrigley Field, as the Cubs hosted the Phillies. With typical Cubs luck, the game was rained out in the fourth inning. They came back the next night to beat the Mets 6-4, at night.

For many years, Hack Wilson's amazing 1930 record for RBI in one season was 190. However, a check of the records by careful researchers found another RBI. In 1999, the commissioner's office officially changed the record to 191. You can look it up!

After that, the Cubs had many good teams—including NL pennant winners in 1929, 1932, 1935, 1938, and 1945—but not quite good enough. They have not been back to the World Series since Manager Charlie Grimm led the 1945 squad that fell to the Tigers in seven games in the Fall Classic (another, though unofficial, name for the World Series).

Chicago has had some tremendous individual talent, however. In 1930, Hack Wilson set the major league record with 191 runs batted in (RBIs) to go along with 56 homers (an NL record that stood 68 years). In 1958, shortstop Ernie Banks became the first player to win a Most Valuable Player (MVP) award while playing for a losing team. "Mr. Cub" won the award again the next year to become the first back-to-back MVP in the NL. Though winning was a rare event for his Cubs, Ernie was always enthusiastic. He was famous for saying, "What a great day for baseball. Let's play two!"

In the 1990s, **charismatic** outfielder Sammy Sosa became a fan favorite and the **scourge** of opposing pitchers. In 1998, Sosa battled the Cardinals' Mark McGwire in a memorable

chase of Roger Maris' single-season record of 61 home runs. Sosa hit 66 that year, just short of McGwire's 70. Also in 1998, rookie right-handed pitcher Kerry Wood took the NL by storm, and equaled a big-league record by striking out 20 batters in a single game. The Cubs finished second in the division and earned a **wild-card** berth that year, but were swept away by the Braves in the postseason.

These days, the Cubs' big star is first baseman Derrek Lee. He had a monster season in 2005, batting .335 with 46 home runs and 107 RBIs before missing much of 2006 to injury.

The Cubs' slugging first baseman Derrek Lee led the NL in hits (199) and batting average (.335) in 2005.

CHAPTER TWO

THE CINCINNATI REDS

The Reds' history is particularly notable for two clubs that took the field more than 100 years apart. One was the first professional team in baseball history in the late 1860s. The other was the "Big Red Machine" that rolled past opponents in the mid-1970s. There have been lots of other great highlights, too, for a franchise whose roots stretch so far back.

The players shown on this scorecard were part of the very first professional baseball team, the 1869 Cincinnati Red Stockings.

Teams had occasionally paid players before, but it was not until the Red Stockings (as the Reds originally were called) of 1869 that a team was made up entirely of professionals. Seven years later, the Red Stockings were a charter member of the National League. They were kicked out of that league in 1880, only to resurface in the rival American Association's first season in 1882. By 1890, Cincinnati was back in the National League, but with a new nickname: the Reds.

Cincinnati had little success in the NL until 1919, when future Hall of Famer Edd Roush and Heinie Groh led the Reds to 96 wins and the team's first pennant. Still, they were a heavy underdog team to the AL champion White Sox. Cincinnati won anyway, five games to three. Afterward, eight White Sox players admitted to taking bribes to lose the World Series on purpose. They were **banned** for life from baseball.

Twenty years later, the Reds won their second NL pennant. Though they fell to the New York Yankees in the World Series, Cincinnati roared to another pennant in 1940. This time, the Reds beat the Detroit Tigers in seven games in the World Series.

The Reds did not win another championship

Catcher Ernie Lombardi, pitcher Bucky Walters, and first baseman Frank McCormick won back-to-back-to-back NL MVP awards from 1938 to 1940. This made the Reds the first team to have different players win the award in consecutive seasons.

The Cubs outfielder Heinie Zimmeman had an interesting name. His real name was Henry, but he was given the nickname of Heinie. At the time, it was sort of an insult to call a person of German descent with that nickname. Today, it would be like giving a person a nickname that made fun of their heritage. Things sure were different back then.

Frank Robinson earned a Triple Crown for Cincinnati in 1966, leading the NL in homers, RBI, and batting average.

for 35 years. But in the meantime, a pair of sluggers entertained the club's fans: Ted Kluszewski and Frank Robinson. Kluszewski, a first baseman, hit 251 homers for the Reds from 1948 to 1957. "Klu" was well known for cutting the sleeves of his jersey to show off his massive muscles. Robinson, one of the first African Americans to play for the Reds, hit 38 homers in his debut in 1956 to win Rookie of the Year honors. In 1961, the superstar outfielder led the Reds to a pennant, hitting .323 with 37 homers and 124 RBIs. He was the NL MVP. The powerful Yankees, though, who won 109 games during the regular season, easily won the World Series in five games.

In 1970, the Reds moved into new Riverfront Stadium, where they soon started building a **dynasty** under Manager Sparky Anderson. Cincinnati won six division titles, four pennants, and two World Series championships in the '70s. "The Big Red Machine," which produced runs

Wily manager Sparky Anderson (left, on the mound removing a pitcher) was the man who pulled the gears of the "Big Red Machine" of the 1970s.

in bunches, had All-Stars up and down the lineup. The batting order featured players such as catcher Johnny Bench, infielders Tony Perez, Joe Morgan, and Pete Rose, and outfielder Ken Griffey.

The 1975 Reds snapped the team's championship drought. Cincinnati won a club-record 108 games that year, then beat the Boston Red Sox in a classic seven-game World Series that ranks as one of the greatest ever. Morgan, the NL MVP, delivered the winning hit in the ninth inning of Game 7. The Reds were perhaps even more dominant the next year. After winning 102 regular-season games, they swept through the postseason without a loss to claim back-to-back World Series crowns. Morgan was the NL MVP again that year. Pitcher Pat Zachary was Rookie of the Year. Rawly Eastwick was the top relief pitcher. Four players won Gold Glove Awards for their fielding. It was one of the best teams of all time.

Rose left the team as a free agent after the '78 season, but he returned in 1984 as a player and manager for the team. On September 11, 1985, he broke Ty Cobb's major league record with his 4,192nd career hit. As a manager, Rose **nurtured** a young team of future stars, including Barry

The 1975 World Series is considered one of the most exciting Fall Classics ever. The Reds took on the AL champion Boston Red Sox in a seven-game thriller. The two teams featured six future Hall of Famers between them and they put on a series of amazing games. Cincinnati was six outs from a title in Game 6 when Bernie Carbo hit a pinch-hit homer for the Red Sox to tie the game. A famous Carlton Fisk homer gave the Red Sox a 12-inning victory. However, the Big Red Machine rolled through the Sox in Game 7. Joe Morgan's ninth-inning RBI gave the Red the championship.

Larkin, Paul O'Neill, and Eric Davis. Rose left the Reds in '89 after he was banned from baseball for betting on games.

Under Manager Lou Piniella, the Reds returned to the World Series in 1990. They swept the favored A's in one of the biggest World Series upsets ever. In 1995, Cincinnati won the first-ever NL Central Division crown (there were no official division winners in the strike-shortened 1994 season). Larkin, a shortstop, was named the NL MVP after hitting .319 with 51 stolen bases. Then in 2000, Reds fans welcomed home Ken Griffey, Jr. The former Seattle Mariners star had played as a young boy on the Riverfront turf during his father's days with the Big Red Machine. At the same time he returned, plans were made to build the Reds a new home. The Great American Ball Park opened on March 31, 2003.

Recent Reds' teams have shown little resemblance to their championship **predecessors**. But Cincinnati currently features a slugger who would fit right in with the Big Red Machine. Six-foot 6-inch, 240-pound Adam Dunn had back-to-back seasons of 40 or more home runs and 100 or more runs batted in (RBI) in 2004 and 2005.

The big and beautiful Great American Ballpark arose in 2003 along the banks of the Ohio River in downtown Cincinnati, signaling a new era in the Reds' history.

CHAPTER THREE

THE HOUSTON ASTROS

A franchise once known mostly for the unique stadium that gave the team its name, the Astros have matured in recent years into a perennial contender for the NL East championship and the league pennant.

Houston got its current nickname after moving into the Astrodome in 1965. The world's first multipurpose, domed stadium was named to honor Houston's importance to the space program and was known as "The Eighth Wonder of the World." The Astrodome was an object of curi-

The logo of the new Houston Colt .45s featured a famous Western handgun; they wisely changed their name to Astros in 1965.

osity for fans and players alike. The club first tried to grow natural grass in the indoor stadium, but when that didn't work out, a new, synthetic turf was invented. Its name, of course, was AstroTurf.

Unfortunately, the Astrodome was of more interest than the play on the field. Beginning with the club's **expansion** season as the Colt .45s in 1962, and despite featuring excellent players such as outfielder Jimmy Wynn, infielder Joe Morgan, and pitcher Larry Dierker, Houston did not finish in the top half of the standings nor post a winning record for the first 10 years of its existence.

In 1972, though, as young outfielder Cesar Cedeno blossomed into a superstar, the Astros forged their first winning season. They went 84–69 and finished in second place in the NL West. Then, mostly under Manager

Superstar second baseman Joe Morgan started his Hall of Fame career as a member of the Houston Astros.

The Astros were on the losing end of one of the most dramatic playoff games ever. In Game 6 of the 1986 World Series, the Astros and Mets played for 16 innings and nearly five hours before the Mets pulled out the victory. It was the longest playoff game in baseball history. The Mets scored three runs in the top of the 16th and it looked like they were finally the NL champs. But the Astros scored two in the bottom of the sixteenth. Finally, Mets closer Jesse Orosco struck out Houston's Kevin Bass with two men on base to end the game and the series.

Bill Virdon, the Astros improved steadily throughout the late 1970s. Finally, in 1980, Houston won the NL West in a one-game playoff with the Dodgers. In the first of many playoff disappointments for Houston, the Astros lost a thrilling National League Championship Series (NLCS) to the Phillies, three games to two. Four of the five contests were decided in extra innings.

Great pitching proved to be the Astros' ticket to the postseason. In 1980, strikeout king Nolan Ryan joined a pitching squad already stocked with Joe Niekro, J. R. Richard, Ken Forsch, and Vern Ruhle. The next year, Ryan pitched the fifth of his record seven career no-hitters and forged an earned-run average (ERA) of 1.69. That helped the Astros return to the playoffs again as second-half champions in the strike-interrupted season, but this time the Dodgers ended their championship hopes in the postseason.

Five years later, the Astros came agonizingly close to their first World Series, winning the West again under rookie manager Hal Lanier. Pitcher Mike Scott led the majors in strikeouts and ERA, winning the Cy Young Award. First baseman Glenn Davis paced the team with 31 homers, the most for an Astros' player in 17 seasons. Scott continued his brilliance in the NLCS against the Mets, winning twice while striking out 19 and yielding only eight hits and one run. Still, New York won a 16-inning thriller in Game 6 to take the series.

The Astros had several good seasons after that, even winning three division titles in a row from 1997 to 1999. Their best team came in 1998, when they won 102 regular-season games. Their potent offense that year featured second baseman Craig Biggio, left fielder Moises Alou, and first baseman Jeff Bagwell. Pitcher Randy Johnson was 10–1 with a 1.28 ERA after coming to Houston in a midseason trade. Still, the Astros fell short of the World Series each time.

In 2000, the Astros moved into Enron Field—their new real-grass ballpark with a retractable roof (meaning it could be mechanically pulled back to open the stadium to the sky). More than 3 million fans came to see a higher-scoring brand of baseball. The Astros set franchise records with 249 home runs and 938 runs in 2000. A division championship in 2001, followed by a three-game sweep by the Braves in the divisional playoffs, left the team zero-for-seven in postseason

Houston in the late 1990s and early 2000s boasted a trio of great players known as the Killer Bs. Craig Biggio was a multi-talented player, seeing time at second base and the outfield while also eventually setting a career record for being hit by pitches. First baseman Jeff Bagwell was one of the NL's most feared sluggers, with six career seasons with 35 or more homers. Outfielder Lance Berkman joined the team in 1999 and has hit more than 200 homers for them.

When the Astros' new ballpark opened, it was named for a huge energy company that paid the Astros to do so. However, a few years later, Enron collapsed and the company bosses were arrested for breaking all sorts of financial laws. Today, the Astros play in Minute Maid Park, after the orange juice company.

Craig Biggio has anchored the Astros lineup, playing both second base and outfield, since he joined the club in 1988.

play. The Astros' new home was renamed Minute Maid Park in 2002. In 2004, Houston earned a wild-card berth and won its first playoff series, beating Atlanta in the opening round. Only a seven-game loss to St. Louis in the NLCS kept the Astros from the World Series.

The next season, though, the Astros turned the tables on the Cardinals. After riding the pitching of veterans Roger Clemens and Andy Pettitte to another wild-card berth, then beating Atlanta in the opening round of the playoffs, Houston upset St. Louis in six games in the NLCS. Not even a four-game sweep at the hands of the Chicago White Sox could dampen the excitement over the club's first NL pennant.

That pennant was just a matter of time. Indeed, the Astros have been the NL Central's most successful team. Before falling off in 2006, Houston finished first or second in 11 of the division's 12 seasons of existence.

Catcher Brad Ausmus and closer Brad Lidge begin the celebration as the Astros wrapped up the 2005 NL championship on their way to their first World Series.

CHAPTER FOUR

THE MILWAUKEE BREWERS

Long-time fans of the Brewers fondly remember the club's formidable teams of the late 1970s and the early 1980s, when Milwaukee fielded the best teams in its history. Younger fans can only patiently hope that such days will soon come again.

The Brewers began as an AL expansion franchise in 1969, but not in Milwaukee. They were located in Seattle and called the Pilots. After just one season in the Pacific Northwest, the team packed up for Milwaukee, which had been without a major-league team since the Braves left for Atlanta following the 1965 season.

The Brewers struggled in their early years in Milwaukee, but a 76–86 season in 1974 was noteworthy for the arrival of 18-year-old shortstop Robin Yount. The future Hall of Famer went on to play his entire career with the Brewers. He retired in 1993 as the team's career leader in almost every batting category, including hits (3,142).

He's just a kid here, but by the time Robin Yount retired, he was a two-time MVP and had crafted a Hall of Fame career.

With designated hitter Larry Hisle (34 home runs) and outfielder Gorman Thomas (32) combining to hit 66 baseballs out of the park, Milwaukee posted its first winning season in 1978. They went 93–69 and finished behind only the Yankees and Red Sox in the AL East. That began a string of six consecutive winning seasons. Most of those teams were known for their home-run hitters. Yount, Thomas, first baseman Cecil Cooper, and outfielder Ben Oglivie helped power a team that topped the major leagues in 1980 in homers, total bases, and slugging percentage. Third baseman Paul Molitor got on base for the big bashers.

Then, various trades brought pitching help. Starter Pete Vuckovich and reliever Rollie Fingers helped the Brewers win a split-season championship in the 1981 strike-shortened year. It was the first time that the franchise had qualified for the postseason. Fingers was brilliant, going 6–3 with a 1.04 ERA and 28 saves. He was the first relief pitcher in history to win both the Cy Young Award and league MVP honors. The Brewers' spectacular season ended in a tightly contested playoff loss to the Yankees.

With Yount, Vuckovich, and Fingers again leading the way, the Brewers won 95 games in 1982.

From 1970 to 1998, the Brewers were run by Allan "Bud" Selig, who then became the commissioner of Major League Baseball. Selig's daughter Wendy Selig-Prieb is currently the Brewers' chairwoman of the board. She is one of the very few women in key executive positions in baseball, or even in all of the major pro sports.

From 1978-1992, versatile Paul Molitor was an anchor of the Brewers offense. Molitor had speed and could bat leadoff, but he could also bat third or fourth and drive in runs. He played six years after leaving Milwaukee, and ended his Hall of Fame career with 3,319 hits and a career .306 average.

After the team got off to a slow start, Manager Buck Rodgers was replaced by hitting coach Harvey Kuenn. "Harvey's Wallbangers" went 72–43 in the season's last four months to capture the AL East crown by one game over the Orioles. With Vuckovich winning the Cy Young Award and Yount (.331 average, 29 homers, 114 RBIs) the MVP, the Brewers became the only AL team to win both major awards in consecutive seasons.

Rollie Fingers made his first mark with the Oakland A's, but he won his only MVP and Cy Young Awards with the Brewers in 1981.

In 2001, the Brewers moved from their longtime home at County Stadium into brand-new Miller Park. The park features a retractable roof, the better to avoid the bad weather that can plague the team in spring and fall. Fans can visit statues to Hall of Famers Hank Aaron and Robin Yount. Team mascot Bernie Brewer used to slide into a giant glass of beer after each homer, but now he just dances.

The Brewers added a big bat in 2006 in the very large person of Prince Fielder. Prince is the son of former home-run king Cecil Fielder, who had 51 homers with Detroit in 1990. Prince is expected to anchor the Brewers lineup for years.

After falling behind the Angels two games to none in the American League Championship Series (ALCS) that year, the Brewers swept the next three games to earn their first trip to the World Series. Against the Cardinals, the Brewers took a three-games-to-two lead to St. Louis's Busch Stadium. But their future division rivals won the last two games to capture the Series.

Milwaukee hasn't been back to the postseason since. The 1987 squad jumped out of the gate with 13 straight wins on its way to a 91-win season. Unfortunately, the team also lost 12 in a row in May to fall out of first place. After winning 92 games under Manager Phil Garner in 1992, the Brewers fell on hard times. Neither a shift to the NL Central in 1998 nor a move into new Miller Park in 2000 made a difference.

In 2005, the Brewers went 81–81 to post their first .500 season in 13 years. Though they failed to build on the optimism of that season in 2006, they have a promising future behind a stable of capable pitching arms. Chris Capuano blossomed into an All-Star in '06, while Doug Davis and Dave Bush teamed with him to give Milwaukee a quality corps of starters on the mound.

Second baseman Bill Hall, shown here turning a double play, led the Brewers with 35 home runs in 2006.

CHAPTER FIVE

THE PITTSBURGH PIRATES

The Pirates have had little success since the current version of the NL Central was formed in 1994. And that's putting it mildly. The fact is, they haven't had a winning season since then (the last time they won more games than they lost was in 1992, when they won the NL East). But don't overlook the rich history of this proud franchise—and the optimism the club has for the immediate future.

Most baseball experts still consider Honus Wagner the greatest all-around shortstop ever, and among baseball's greatest players at any position.

Honus Wagner was a barrel-chested, bow-legged man with power and surprising speed and agility. He hit .300 or better in an amazing 15 straight seasons and won eight batting titles on his way to a lifetime .327 average. Wagner also repeated led the NL in stolen bases, RBI, doubles, triples, and total bases.

The list of truly great third baseman is one of the shortest position lists in the game. One name that usually makes that list, but that few fans recognize, is Pirates' Hall of Famer Harold "Pie" Traynor. From 1920 through 1937, he was one of the league's best fielders, while also knocking in 100 RBI seven times and finishing with a career .320 average.

The franchise's roots date back to 1882, when the club began play in the American Association. The club was originally named the Alleghenys after one of two rivers (the other being the Monongahela) that merge in the Steel City to form the Ohio River. In 1887, Pittsburgh joined the fledgling National League and lured second baseman Louis Bierbauer away from the Philadelphia Athletics of the American Association. The A's cried foul, accusing the cross-state team of "pirating" their team. Pittsburgh kept the player and got a new nickname, too.

In the early 1900s, the Pirates were the NL's dominant team. They were led by shortstop Honus Wagner, who was one of the greatest players in baseball history. With Wagner batting .355 and driving in 101 runs, the Pirates won their third consecutive NL pennant in 1903 before losing to the AL's Boston Pilgrims (now the Red Sox) in the first World Series. Six years later, Wagner helped the Pirates win their first World Series in seven games over the Detroit Tigers.

The next title came 16 years later. With more future Hall of Famers in the lineup such as Max Carey, Kiki Cuyler, and Pie Traynor, the Pirates returned to the World Series in 1925. Down three games to one, Pittsburgh rallied to defeat the Washington Senators and their ace, Walter "Big Train" Johnson. A strong Pirates team became even stronger with the addition of the Waner brothers: Lloyd "Little Poison" and Paul "Big Poison." They took the NL crown again two years later, only to have the misfortune of facing maybe the best team in baseball history. The fabled '27 Yankees, with their "Murderers Row" lineup featuring Babe Ruth and Lou Gehrig, swept the Series in four straight games.

For most of the next three decades, the Pirates had little success. There were several outstanding individual achievements, however. Slugger Ralph Kiner won or shared the league home run title for a record seven straight seasons from 1946 to 1952. First baseman Dale Long set a mark in '56 by hitting a home run in eight straight games. And pitcher Harvey Haddix made history on May 26, 1959, by pitching 12 perfect innings against the Milwaukee Braves. Unfortunately for Haddix and the Pirates, the no-hitter and the game were lost in the 13th inning.

In 1960, though, Haddix and his teammates

How did the Waner brothers get their unusual nicknames? The most popular story tracks to Brooklyn, where a loud fan, in that New York City section's well-known accent, asked "Who is dat little poison?" meaning, "Who is that little person?" Soon, the Waners were Big Poison and Little Poison . . . and it had nothing to do with dangerous chemicals!

Ralph Kiner was a feared slugger. One year after he led the league in home runs, he asked for a raise in salary. The unsuccessful Pirates owner turned him down, saying, "If you don't like it, we finished last with you and we can finish last without you!"

capped a tremendous season with an unforgettable World Series performance. Pittsburgh again faced a Yankees team rich with stars such as Mickey Mantle, Roger Maris, Yogi Berra, and Whitey Ford. In its three losses in the Series, Pittsburgh was humbled by a combined score of 38–3. But the Pirates also won three close games, leading up to Game Seven at Pittsburgh's Forbes Field. There, Bill Mazeroski ended a seesaw struggle with a leadoff homer in the bottom of the ninth, giving the Pirates a 10–9 victory. The second baseman's blast remains the only walk-off home run in a World Series Game 7.

Accompanied by his third-base coach and a very eager fan, Bill Mazeroski rounds third and heads for home after hitting a homer to win the 1960 World Series.

Roberto Clemente was a young outfielder who hit .310 in the 1960 World Series. Eleven years later, he led the Pirates back to the Series, against Baltimore. Clemente was the MVP of that Series, hitting .414 as the Pirates prevailed four games to three. The beloved 12-time All-Star finished his career by collecting his 3,000th hit on the last day of the 1972 season. Three months later, he died in a plane crash on his way to help earthquake victims in Nicaragua. Clemente's legacy is the large number of major league players today who come from Latin America.

Leadership of the Pirates passed to first baseman Willie "Pops" Stargell. In his 21 seasons, Stargell racked up more homers (475), RBIs (1,540), and extra-base hits (953) than any other player in the Pirates' history. In 1979, at 39, he captained the Pirates ship to another World Series title. In the process, he pulled off a very rare triple: He was the NL season co-MVP, the NLCS MVP, and the World Series MVP.

The incomparable Roberto Clemente was the heart and soul of the Pirates for more than 14 seasons. His tragic death in 1972 still resonates in baseball today.

After failing to reach the postseason at any time during the 1980s, the Pirates returned to power a decade later, winning three straight NL East titles from 1990 to 1992. However, they could not get to the World Series, losing once to the Reds and twice to the Braves. The third loss was the toughest. The Braves scored three runs in the bottom of the ninth to win Game 7 of the 1992 NLCS. That was the last real success the Pirates have enjoyed.

Jim Tracy, who guided the Dodgers to a division championship in 2004, took over as manager in 2006. Though the Pirates failed to live up to the hopes his hiring generated, the season had several highlights. One was the continued emergence of outfielder Jason Bay, who started in the All-Star Game played in Pittsburgh's PNC Park that year. Another All-Star, infielder Freddy Sanchez, hit a career-best .344 in '06.

Freddy Sanchez started the 2006 season on the bench; by the end of the season, he was the surprise NL batting champion.

CHAPTER SIX

THE ST. LOUIS CARDINALS

No other player in baseball today commands the attention of opposing pitchers quite like Cardinals first baseman Albert Pujols. St. Louis fans and the national media call him "Prince Albert." That's because he's as close as it gets to baseball royalty.

Pujols, the son of former major leaguer Luis Pujols, was just 21 when he debuted on Opening Day in 2001. Albert Pujols made an immediate and huge impact, batting .329 with 37 home runs and 130

Roger "Rajah" Hornsby holds the 20th-century record for single-season batting average with a .424 mark in 1924.

St. Louis joined the NL twice: in 1876 for two seasons and again in 1892. From 1892 to 1898, the franchise was known as the Browns. Then in 1899, it was the Perfectos. Finally, in 1900, it became the Cardinals and that's the name that has stuck all these years.

Among Rogers Hornsby's many other great accomplishments:

- Only winner of two Triple Crowns (leading league in RBI, HR, and average)
- From 1920-25, batted at least .370 each season
- Five seasons with 125 or more RBI
- Led NL in slugging average nine times and on-base percentage 10 times

RBIs as a rookie. He went on to average 40 home runs and 124 RBIs in his first five seasons, and in 2005 he was named the NL's most valuable player for the first time.

Pujols is the latest in a long line of superstars in the Cardinals' history. Hall of Famers such as Rogers Hornsby, Jay "Dizzy" Dean, Enos Slaughter, Stan Musial, Lou Brock, and Bob Gibson are part of the heritage for a franchise that began play in 1876. The Cardinals have won more World Series championships (nine) than any other franchise in the NL, and more than any other team but the New York Yankees (26) in all of baseball.

Hornsby, a second baseman, is one of only two NL players to hit more than .400 for a season, a feat he managed three times. His .424 average in 1924 is the modern-day record for highest average over a season. As a manager and player in 1926, he led the Cards to their first World Series title.

The next World Series win came in 1931. Then, three years later, Dean was the cornerstone of the famous "Gashouse Gang" that carried the Cardinals to another championship. Dean and his brother Paul "Daffy" Dean, Frankie Frisch, Pepper

Martin, Leo Durocher, and more formed a team that was as zany, cocky, and fiery as it was talented.

Two more stars were important components of three World Series winners in the 1940s. Enos "Country" Slaughter scored the winning run in Game 7 of the 1946 World Series from first base on a single in what has become known as his "mad dash." But Stan "The Man" Musial might well be the best, and most popular, player in the Cardinals' history. In his 22-year career with St. Louis, the slugger earned seven batting crowns, three MVP awards, and a record 24 All-Star Game selections (some years two All-Star Games were played).

After beating the Red Sox in the exciting 1946 World Series, the Cardinals didn't win another crown until 1964. By that time, pitching was the name of the game in baseball. And the most dominant pitcher in the majors was the Cards' hard-throwing right-hander Bob Gibson. He won 19 games for the club's 1964 World Series winners, and 13 games in only 24 starts for the '76 champs. Then, in 1968, he was nearly untouchable. That year, he recorded 22 wins, 28 complete games, 13 shutouts, a 1.12 ERA, and 268 strikeouts. He won both the Cy Young

During Game 7 of the 1934 World Series, Cardinals star Joe "Ducky" Medwick infuriated Detroit players and fans with a hard slide into the Tigers' third baseman. Angry fans threw fruit, eggs, and vegetables at him until baseball commissioner Kenesaw Landis ejected him from the game to calm things down. The Cards won the game 11–0 to take the series.

Bob Gibson's 1968 success highlighted the "Year of the Pitcher." Pitching was so dominant that year that for the 1969 season the league lowered the mound by five inches, from 15 to 10. This helped batters see the ball a bit better and batting averages and offense began to rise again.

and MVP awards, although St. Louis' bid for another title ended in a taut seven-game loss to the Detroit Tigers in the World Series.

Another star of the '60s-era Cardinals was speedy outfielder Lou Brock. From 1965 to 1976, the six-time All-Star averaged 65 steals per season and won eight stolen base titles. Brock set a season record (since broken) of 118 steals in 1974.

The Cards returned to the World Series three times in the 1980s under Manager Whitey Herzog, winning in 1982 and losing in '85 and '87. All three series were tense, seven-game affairs. Taking advantage of the fast artificial turf at Busch Stadium, Herzog's teams featured speed up and down the lineup. The road-running Redbirds showed how effective speed and defense could be. In fact, they won the 1982

Safe . . . again! Lou Brock set new standards for base stealers during his Hall of Fame career, spent mostly with St. Louis. He stole a then-record 118 bases in 1974.

World Series despite hitting the fewest home runs in the majors! The heart and soul of those Cardinals teams was shortstop Ozzie Smith. "The Wizard of Oz" won 13 straight Gold Glove Awards. He made the difficult plays look routine and the impossible plays look spectacular. Fans loved Ozzie, and his defensive wizardry earned the Hall of Famer 15 All-Star selections.

In 1998, a different kind of Cardinals player captured the nation's attention. Mark McGwire, a huge, slugging first baseman acquired from Oakland the year before, launched an assault on one of baseball's most famous records. Roger Maris's home run mark of 61 (set in 1961) had seemed out of reach for years. But McGwire went after it from the season's opening bell. Finally, on September 8, he connected for number 62 off the Cubs' Steve Trachsel. With a homer in the season's final game, McGwire closed with 70. Only McGwire and San Francisco's

Ozzie Smith dazzled fans with his Gold Glove fielding exploits. He added a bit of fun by occasionally performing a backflip like this on his way to his position.

Barry Bonds (with a new record 73 in 2001) have ever hit 70 or more homers in a season.

In 1996, Tony LaRussa took over as manager and led the club to six division titles in the next 11 seasons. The 2004 team won 105 regular-season games before being swept by Boston in the World Series. Two years later, the Cardinals won only 83 games, but again ended up on top of the NL Central. In the playoffs, they defeated the Padres and Mets. Facing the powerful Tigers in the World Series, St. Louis won its 10th baseball championship. They had the fewest regular-season wins of any World Series champ. But they were still the champs!

Albert Pujols (and his son A.J.) join manager Tony LaRussa (right) in joyfully holding up the 2006 World Series championship trophy.

STAT STUFF

TEAM RECORDS (THROUGH 2006)

Team	All-time Record	World Series Titles (Most Recent)	Number of Times in the Postseason	Top Manager (Wins)
Chicago Cubs	9,900–9,382	2 (1908)	14	Cap Anson (1,283)
Cincinnati	9,600–9,286	5 (1990)	12	Sparky Anderson (863)
Houston	3,579–3,583	0	8	Bill Virdon (544)
Milwaukee*	2,836–3,187	0	2	Phil Garner (585)
Pittsburgh	9,556–9,291	5 (1979)	14	Fred Clarke (1,422)
St. Louis	9,765–9,111	10 (2006)	22	Red Schoendienst (1,041)

**includes Seattle*

NATIONAL LEAGUE CENTRAL CAREER LEADERS (THROUGH 2006)

CHICAGO

Category	Name (Years with Team)	Total
Batting Average	Bill Madlock (1974–76)	.336
Home Runs	Sammy Sosa (1992–2004)	545
RBI	Cap Anson (1876–1897)	1,879
Stolen Bases	Frank Chance (1898–1912)	400
Wins	Charlie Root (1926–1941)	201
Saves	Lee Smith (1980–87)	180
Strikeouts	Ferguson Jenkins (1966–1973, 1982–83)	2,038

CINCINNATI

Category	Name (Years with Team)	Total
Batting Average	Cy Seymour (1902–06)	.332
Home Runs	Johnny Bench (1967–1983)	389
RBI	Johnny Bench (1967–1983)	1,376
Stolen Bases	Joe Morgan (1972–1979)	406
Wins	Eppa Rixey (1921–1933)	179
Saves	Danny Graves (1997–2005)	182
Strikeouts	Jim Maloney (1960–1970)	1,592

HOUSTON

Category	Name (Years with Team)	Total
Batting Average	Lance Berkman (1999–2006)	.304
Home Runs	Jeff Bagwell (1991–2006)	449
RBI	Jeff Bagwell (1991–2006)	1,529
Stolen Bases	Cesar Cedeno (1970–1981)	487
Wins	Joe Niekro (1975–1985)	144
Saves	Billy Wagner (1995–2006)	225
Strikeouts	Nolan Ryan (1980–88)	1,866

MILWAUKEE

Category	Name (Years with Team)	Total
Batting Average	Jeff Cirillo (1994–99)	.307
Home Runs	Robin Yount (1974–1993)	251
RBI	Robin Yount (1974–1993)	1,406
Stolen Bases	Paul Molitor (1978–1992)	412
Wins	Jim Slaton (1971–77, 1979–1983)	117
Saves	Dan Plesac (1986–1992)	133
Strikeouts	Teddy Higuera (1985–1994)	1,081

MORE STAT STUFF

NATIONAL LEAGUE CENTRAL CAREER LEADERS (THROUGH 2006)

PITTSBURGH

Category	Name (Years with Team)	Total
Batting Average	Paul Waner (1926–1940)	.340
Home Runs	Willie Stargell (1962–1982)	475
RBI	Willie Stargell (1962–1982)	1,540
Stolen Bases	Max Carey (1910–1926)	688
Wins	Wilbur Cooper (1912–1924)	202
Saves	Roy Face (1953–1968)	188
Strikeouts	Bob Friend (1951–1965)	1,682

ST. LOUIS

Category	Name (Years with Team)	Total
Batting Average	Rogers Hornsby (1915–1926, 1933)	.359
Home Runs	Stan Musial (1941–1963)	475
RBI	Stan Musial (1941–1963)	1,951
Stolen Bases	Lou Brock (1964–1979)	888
Wins	Bob Gibson (1959–1975)	251
Saves	Jason Isringhausen (2002–2006)	173
Strikeouts	Bob Gibson (1959–1975)	3,117

GLOSSARY

banned—prevented from taking part, usually forever or for a long period of time, because of a rules violation

charismatic—having a bubbly and attractive personality

charter member—a group that is among the very first members of a larger organization

dynasty—a team that wins a number of championships in a short period of time

expansion—making larger; in this case, making a league larger by adding a team

nurtured—helped to grow or improve; provided direction for young people

pennant—the championship of each league in baseball

predecessors—people or groups that came before

scourge—a long-term enemy or troublemaker

wild-card—in baseball, a team that finishes in second place in its division but still earns a spot in the playoffs

TIMELINE

1869 The Cincinnati Red Stockings are baseball's first all-professional team.

1876 The NL begins play, with Chicago, Cincinnati, and St. Louis among the charter franchises.

1882 The Pittsburgh Alleghenys are formed; they become known as the Pirates in 1891.

1908 The Cubs win the World Series for the second consecutive year.

1924 St. Louis second baseman Rogers Hornsby bats .424, still a big-league record.

1926 The Cardinals win the first of their NL-best nine World Series titles.

1962 The Houston Colt .45s join the NL as an expansion team (a new franchise); they become known as the Astros in 1965.

1969 The Seattle Pilots debut in the AL West; one year later, they move to Milwaukee and become the Brewers.

1975 The Cincinnati Reds win the first of back-to-back World Series.

1979 First baseman Willie Stargell leads the Pirates to their fifth World Series championship.

1980 The Astros win a division title and make the playoffs for the first time.

1982 The Brewers win their first and, so far, only pennant in club history; they lose in the World Series.

1998 The Brewers move from the AL to the NL.

Cardinals first baseman Mark McGwire blasts 70 home runs to break Roger Maris's single-season record; McGwire outduels Chicago's Sammy Sosa, who finishes with 66 homers.

2006 St. Louis Cardinals win their 10th World Series title.

FOR MORE INFORMATION

BOOKS

Christopher, Matt. *At the Plate with Sammy Sosa.* Boston: Little Brown & Co., 1999.

Doherty, Craig A., and Katherine M. Doherty. *The Houston Astrodome.* Woodbridge, Conn.: Blackbirch Press, 1997.

Rambeck, Richard. *Milwaukee Brewers: AL East.* Mankato, Minn.: Creative Education, 1992.

Stewart, Mark. *Mark McGwire: Home Run King.* New York: Children's Press, 1999.

ON THE WEB

Visit our home page for lots of links about the National League Central teams: ***http://www.childsworld.com/links***
Note to Parents, Teachers, and Librarians: We routinely check our Web links to make sure they're safe, active sites—so encourage your readers to check them out!

INDEX

ABOUT THE AUTHOR

John Silbaugh is a middle-school teacher in Colorado, where he lives with his wife and three daughters. A lifelong fan of the Pirates, John has worked as a tour guide at Coors Field, the home park of the Colorado Rockies. This is his first book.